HOW TO SWALLOW A PIG

A

STEVE JENKINS & ROBIN PAGE

STEP-BY-STEP ADVICE FROM THE ANIMAL KINGDOM

HOUGHTON MIFFLIN HARCOURT   BOSTON NEW YORK

So, you want to learn how to swallow a pig. You've come to the right place. Follow these step-by-step instructions, and soon you'll acquire the dining skills of a large snake. But maybe you're not quite ready to gulp down a hairy four-legged animal. Don't worry—there are lots of other useful techniques you can master. After all, you never know when you might need to spin a web, disguise yourself as a jellyfish, battle a sheep, or catch a wildebeest. Just take it slow, and remember: practice makes perfect.

How to
Trap Fish
Like a Humpback Whale

A **humpback whale** is the size of a school bus, and it can consume thousands of fish in one meal. Whales are mammals, so they breathe air. This allows them to catch fish in an unusual way: with a bubble net.

If you'd like to try it yourself, here's how you go about it:

❶ Find some fish.

The first step is locating a school of fish. Some of these schools include millions of herring or sardines.

❷ Tell your friends.

Call any humpbacks in the area and let them know you've located dinner.

❸ Slap the surface.

Whacking the water with your tail frightens the fish and makes them swim closer together. If you don't have a tail, ask one of the whales for help.

❹ Swim in circles.

Join the whales in circling beneath the fish while blowing a steady stream of bubbles. Herd the fish together by swimming in smaller and smaller circles.

❺ Gulp!

Take turns swimming straight up through the cluster of fish. Open your mouth wide and swallow as many fish as you can in one gulp.

How to
Sew
Like a Tailorbird

The **tailorbird** gets its name from the ingenious way it makes its nest. A female tailorbird constructs the nest, but her male companion may help her collect material for it. Here's how it's done:

❶ Choose a leaf.

You'll need a large green leaf. It's best to choose one in a safe, out-of-the-way spot.

❷ Wrap the leaf.

Bend the edges of the leaf together by wrapping it in long strands of spider web silk.

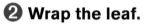

❺ Line your nest.

Collect soft plant fibers, insect cocoons, or spider web silk. Use these to line your nest and make it soft and comfortable. Now you're ready to lay your eggs.

❸ Use your beak as a needle.

Poke holes in two edges of the leaf with your sharp beak.

❹ Find thread.

Use plant fibers, grass, or spider silk to sew the edges of the nest together. Push this thread through each pair of holes, then fluff out the ends to keep the stitches from coming loose.

How to

Repel Insects

Like a Capuchin

Capuchin monkeys live in the rainforest among lots of mosquitoes, flies, and other biting insects. Insects can make a monkey's life miserable, but these clever primates have found ways to protect themselves. If you want to follow their lead, here's what you do:

❶ Get together.

Capuchins make their insect-repelling sessions a social occasion. You can join in.

❷ Grab a millipede.

Some millipedes defend themselves by excreting poison through their skin. The powerful chemicals they produce also repel most insects.

❺ Crush some piper leaves.

The leaves of the piper vine also contain chemicals that repel insects. If a millipede isn't doing the job—or if you can't find one—try crushing a few piper leaves and rubbing them all over your fur. Now you're protected against those pesky insects.

❸ Pop the millipede in your mouth.

Ugh! This burns and it tastes terrible, but rolling the millipede around with your tongue encourages it to release its toxins.

❹ Rub the millipede on your fur.

And be sure to share your millipede with any monkeys that don't have their own.

How to
Woo a Ewe
Like a Mountain Sheep

A female **bighorn sheep** is called a ewe. When two male sheep, or rams, want to impress a ewe, they fight each other. The victor wins the affections of the female. Warning: Try this at your own risk. It could give you a very bad headache.

❶ Look around.

See that big ram over there? He's your rival. Look—he's headed this way . . .

❷ Stand your ground.

Try to look tough. Maybe you can get him to back down.

❸ Time to tussle.

Better start pushing and bumping this guy. Because he's going to do it to you.

❹ Now it's getting serious.

Rear up on your hind legs, charge your opponent, and smash your head into his.

❺ Take a break.

If your skull is as thick as a mountain sheep's, you won't suffer any permanent damage. And if the other guy backs down, you have a new girlfriend.

How to
Crack a Nut
Like a Crow

Crows are intelligent birds, and they have learned to crack nuts by carrying them into the air and dropping them on rocks or pavement. But some nuts are too tough, and even this treatment won't break them open. In some places, crows have found a solution.

It's probably best not to try this technique until you learn how to fly.

❶ Find a nut.

A walnut or other tough-shelled nut is a good choice.

❷ Select your perch.

Find a spot near a traffic signal above a busy road.

❸ Drop your nut.

Choose a place where the nut will get run over by a car or truck.

❺ Enjoy!

Now you can swoop down, eat your nut, and take off before the light changes again.

❹ Wait for the light to change.

Don't try to collect the pieces of your smashed snack until the light has changed and traffic has stopped.

How to
Build a Dam
Like a Beaver

The **beaver** is an expert animal engineer. Working with its family members, it dams a stream to create a pond where it can store food and build a home.

Here are instructions for making your own dam the way a beaver would:

❶ Find a stream.

The best choice is water that flows year-round but doesn't move too fast.

❷ Chop down some trees.

Using your front teeth, gnaw through the trunks of a few trees. Try to make the trees fall across the stream, where they will form the foundation of your dam.

❺ Take a swim in your new pond.

And take a break—next you'll be building a lodge.

❸ Collect sticks and mud.

This job will go faster if you can persuade a beaver family to pitch in.

❹ Complete your dam.

Use the sticks and mud you've gathered to fill in the holes in your dam.

How to
Disguise Yourself
Like an Octopus

There are many different kinds of octopus. All of them can alter the color and texture of their skin to blend in with their surroundings. The **mimic octopus**, however, takes things a step further. It imitates other sea creatures to frighten or confuse predators.

Be prepared for this to take flexibility, creativity, and lots of practice.

❶ Watch out for danger.

Lots of animals want to make a meal of a little octopus.

❷ Choose a disguise.

Pick a threatening or unappetizing animal to imitate.

❸ Mimic a sea snake.

Change your skin by covering it with black and yellow stripes. Then extend two arms in opposite directions and wriggle through the water. With luck, your attacker will mistake you for a deadly sea snake.

4 Perhaps a lionfish . . .

Hover in the water, spread your arms, and let them trail behind you. Now you look like a lionfish, a colorful fish with poison-tipped fins.

5 How about a flatfish?

Flatfish spend their time resting on the sea floor or swimming just above it. Some of these fish are poisonous, so predators avoid them. To imitate a flatfish, pull all of your arms together, flatten your body, and glide along the ocean floor.

6 Don't forget the jellyfish!

Most sea creatures avoid jellyfish and their stinging tentacles. This one's easy: Hover in the water with your arms trailing behind you. Every so often, rise to the surface, then slowly descend.

How to

Hunt

Like a Reddish Egret

The **reddish egret** hunts small fish that hide among rocks and plants in shallow water. The egret has some effective techniques for catching these fish. These tricks can work for you, too, but you'll have to get your feet wet.

① Look.

As you wade through the water, watch for places that would make good hiding spots for fish.

② Splash.

Begin to hop about, splashing and making lots of noise.

④ Shade.

When the sun is shining, reflections can make it difficult to see beneath the surface. Raise your wings to shade your eyes, and you'll be able to spot and spear more fish.

③ Grab.

With your long, sharp beak, grab any frightened fish that dart into open water. When you catch one, toss it into the air and swallow it head first.

How to

Build a Nest

Like a Wasp

Paper wasps fashion their nest from chewed wood fibers mixed with saliva. The nest contains many individual cells, and each cell holds a developing wasp larva. Even though it is made of paper, the nest is waterproof.

If you want to make a paper wasp nest, get ready to do a lot of chewing.

❶ Find a good spot.

A protected area is best, perhaps under a porch or beneath a large tree branch.

❷ Start making "paper."

You'll need to find a source of wood, such as an old log or unpainted fence. To make paper pulp, bite off a small piece of wood and chew it thoroughly, mixing it with your saliva.

❸ Attach your nest.

Attach a bit of the soggy paper pulp to the spot you've chosen. This pulp forms the stem that will anchor your nest.

❻ The finishing touch.

Using a gland on your abdomen, apply a special liquid to the stem that supports the nest. This liquid repels ants, preventing them from crawling into the nest and eating the eggs and larvae.

❺ Add the "umbrella."

Use more paper pulp to cover the whole nest in a protective paper wrapping. Be sure to leave a small hole at the bottom for coming and going.

❹ Add cells.

You'll need to construct lots of hexagonal (six-sided) cells. This shape is ideal because it allows the cells to fit together neatly without any wasted space. The wasp queen lays an egg in each cell, where it hatches into a larva and eventually becomes an adult wasp.

How to
Spin a Web
Like a Spider

The **barn spider** follows a careful plan when it builds its web. You can build a web the same way. Before you start, however, you'll need to find a protected place to build your web, and—this is the tricky part—you'll have to learn how to spin silk threads.

❶ Cast a line.

Once you've found the right spot, cast a single silk thread into the air. If you're lucky, the breeze will catch it and it will snag on a nearby branch or other object.

❷ Make a loop.

Walk across the first thread and spin another that droops to form a U.

❸ Turn your U into a Y.

Drop a line from the bottom of the loose thread and tighten it to make a Y shape.

❹ Frame your web.

Spin threads that will form the borders of your web.

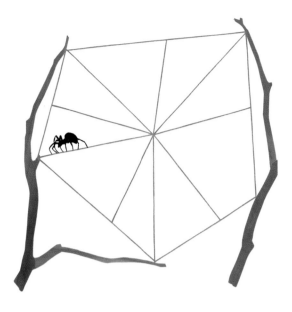

❺ Spin threads from the center to the edges.

These lines are called radii (*ray-dee-ahy*). They will form the framework for your web and give you unsticky threads to walk on.

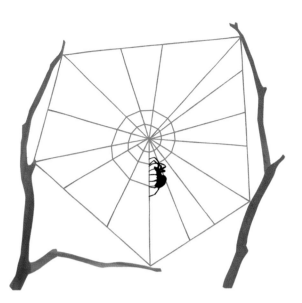

❻ Make a spiral.

Working from the inside out, make a spiral of silk. So far, none of the threads you've spun are sticky.

❼ Get sticky.

Now work your way back to the center, laying down sticky threads. The original spiral will be your path, and you'll recycle it by eating it as you go.

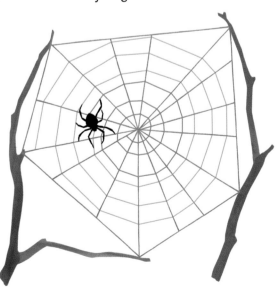

❽ Wait for dinner.

Now you can rest. Sit in the center of your new web and wait for an insect to blunder into your trap.

How to
Decorate
Like a Bowerbird

A male **satin bowerbird** fashions a nest of sticks and twigs, then decorates it. When the nest, or bower, is finished, a female bowerbird will inspect it. If she likes what she sees, she may choose the nest builder as her mate.

If you'd like to make your own bower, here's a tip: satin bowerbirds are especially fond of the color blue.

❶ Choose a site.

Building your nest in a forest clearing is a good bet.

❷ Collect sticks.

You'll need a lot of sticks. Once you have a good supply, begin to weave them into a "U" shape.

❸ Find colorful objects.

When the nest structure is complete, gather lots of colorful stones, shells, or flower petals. Man-made objects also work well. Bowerbirds have decorated with bottle caps, jewelry, bits of broken glass—even eyeglasses and fountain pens.

❹ Organize them.

Arrange your colorful objects to make a path leading into and out of the nest.

❺ Make your own paint.

Chew up berries, mix them with your saliva, and use your beak to paint the inside of your bower blue.

❻ Wait patiently.

When a female bowerbird shows up, she'll expect you to present your work with a dance. But that's another project.

How to
Warn of Danger
Like a Vervet Monkey

Vervet monkeys live in large groups, or troops. They have many enemies, so every monkey in the troop keeps an eye out for danger. The monkeys make distinct cries to warn of different predators. If you want to warn of danger like a vervet, you'll have to learn several alarm calls.

❶ Stay alert.

Along with every other member of the troop, you must watch for dangerous animals.

❷ Danger from the air.

Eagles are one of the deadliest vervet predators. They can swoop down and snatch you—or some other member of your troop—from the treetops. If you spot one of these birds, give the eagle alarm. All the monkeys will drop to a lower branch of the tree and look up.

❹ Slithering danger.

Snakes can attack from the ground or the branches of a tree, so when vervets hear the snake alarm, they freeze and look all around. If you give an alarm call, be sure it's the correct one, or you could be sending a monkey into danger.

❸ Danger from the ground.

Leopards are another deadly threat, especially when you are on the ground. Give the leopard alarm cry, then leap up into the branches along with the other monkeys.

How to
Farm
Like a Leaf-Cutter Ant

Leaf-cutter ants are farmers. The members of a colony work together to raise a crop of fungus as food. If you want to help out, you'll need lots of energy and a pair of sharp jaws.

❶ Hunting for leaves.

Set off in a line with thousands of ants to search for the right kind of leaves. You don't want to get lost, so as you march leave a chemical trail to guide you back to the nest.

❷ Snip, snip.

Once you've found a good source of leaves, use your scissorlike jaws to cut them into pieces.

❸ Homeward bound.

Each ant heads home with a piece of leaf in its jaws. Leaf-cutters can carry loads that weigh ten times as much as they do—just do your best.

❹ Fertilize the farm.

The colony's fungus farm is grown in a large underground cavern. Here other ants chew the leaves to a pulp that is used to fertilize the fungus. The leaves themselves are not eaten.

❺ A fungus feast.

You've worked hard—treat yourself to a delicious fungus snack.

How to
Catch a Meal
Like a Crocodile

The **crocodile** moves swiftly in water, but many of the animals it hunts live on land. Here the crocodile is more awkward, and its prey can often get away if it sees the croc coming. As a result, these huge reptiles have developed tricky ways of hunting. It helps to be sneaky if you want to catch a meal like a croc.

❶ Pretend to be a log.

Find a spot near a riverbank and lie quietly in the water with just your eyes and nostrils above the surface. If you stay motionless, your prey may not notice you, or it might mistake you for a floating log.

❷ Get ready.

A wildebeest is approaching to take a drink. Gather yourself . . .

❸ Lunge!

With a thrust of your tail, lunge from the water with your mouth open wide. If you can grab the wildebeest, drag it into the water and hold it under until it drowns (no one said this would be pretty).

❹ Another try.

If you couldn't catch the wildebeest, here's another trick. Find some sticks and lie motionless with them balanced on your nose. Why sticks? Wading birds such as egrets collect sticks to build their nests.

❺ Dinner.

When an egret lands nearby to pick up one of your sticks, you know what to do.

How to
Defend Yourself
Like an Armadillo

Most of the **nine-banded armadillo's** body is covered with bony plates, but it has a soft, vulnerable belly. Coyotes, foxes, jaguars, and other predators often try to make a meal of this little mammal, so it has come up with some clever ways of defending itself.

The next time you're attacked by a predator, try borrowing from the armadillo's bag of tricks.

❶ Freeze!

Many predators don't notice prey unless it's moving, so holding perfectly still can be a good survival tactic.

❷ Run.

They may not look like athletes, but armadillos can move quickly. So can you. If freezing doesn't work, don't just sit there.

❸ Dig.

Start digging a hole with your long claws. Work quickly, and you'll soon have a snug burrow to hide in.

❻ Hunker down.

If all else fails, pull in your head and feet and hope your armor persuades the attacker to give up.

❺ Leap.

Try jumping several feet straight up into the air. This can startle even the fiercest predator and give you time to escape.

❹ Swim.

You're a good swimmer. And not every predator likes to get wet.

How to
Catch an Insect
Like an Ant Lion

Or, more accurately, like an ant lion larva. An adult **ant lion** resembles a dragonfly and feeds on pollen and nectar. But before this insect is mature—when it's still in its larval form—it is a vicious predator. Ant lion larvae dig pits to trap ants and other small creatures. Sound like fun? Here's how you go about it:

❶ Find a patch of fine, dry soil.

This is where you'll excavate your pit.

❸ Hide.

When your pit is finished, bury yourself at the bottom, facing upward.

❷ Use your head.

Make your head into a shovel, tossing out loose soil as you move backwards in a tightening spiral. Your pit will grow deeper and deeper.

❹ Seize your prey.

When an ant or other insect tumbles into your pit, it will try to scramble out. If you've made a good trap, your victim will keep slipping to the bottom. Grab it with your jaws and inject it with poison.

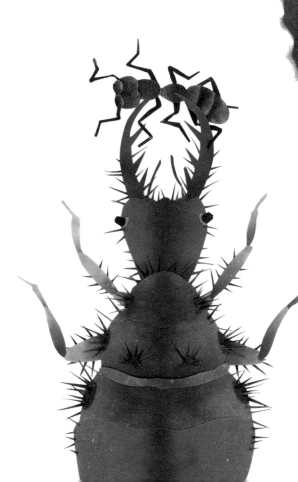

❺ Have dinner.

Next, suck all of the juices out of your prey. When you've finished, toss the dead insect away, repair any damage to your pit, and wait for the next victim.

How to
Dance
Like a Grebe

The **western grebe** spends most of its time paddling around lakes and marshes. At mating time, male and female grebes perform an elaborate dance. This dance will be easier for you to master if you have a beak, wings, and wide, flat toes.

❶ A gift of weeds.

If you are a guy, start things off by offering a female grebe a gift of water plants. If you're a girl, you can decide whether or not to accept the gift.

❷ I do what you do.

The next step is to imitate each other's gestures. For example, you might raise and lower your head. If there is romance in the air, the other bird will copy you.

❸ Footsie.

If your partner raises a foot and waves it in the air, you should do the same. This is easy for a western grebe, because its feet are located at the back of its body rather than underneath, like those of most birds.

❹ The rush.

The final step in the dance is called rushing, and it is the most fun. Position yourself side-by-side with your partner, then start paddling your feet as hard as you can. If you do this properly, you'll rise out of the water and sprint across the surface, splashing water in all directions.

How to
Swallow a Pig
Like a Python

The **python** is a constrictor. It squeezes its prey to death, then swallows it whole. A large python can gulp down an animal as big as a pig or deer. If you want to eat a meal that size, you'll have to do a few things that you're probably not used to.

❶ Hide.

Lie quietly, perhaps draped over the branch of a tree.

❷ Wait . . .

If you are patient, a wild pig or other large animal might wander by. Look, here comes one now!

❸ Attack!

This is your chance. Lunge at your victim and grab it with your sharp, backwards-pointing fangs. Quickly wrap your coils around its body.

❹ Squeeze.

Squeeze hard. Soon the pig won't be able to take a breath, and it will suffocate.

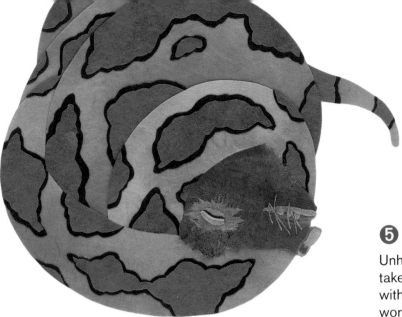

❺ Swallow.

Unhinge your jaw (this takes practice). Starting with the head, begin to work the pig down your throat.

❻ Rest.

Once the pig is completely swallowed, take a nap. You won't have to eat again for several months.

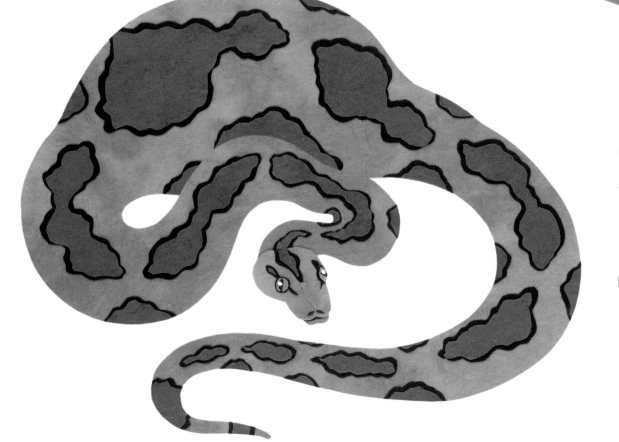

Congratulations! You've learned some useful tricks. If you had trouble with a few of them, don't worry – just keep working at it.
If you'd like to take a break from nest building and pig swallowing to find out more about the creatures in this book, turn the page.

A **humpback whale** can reach 60 feet (18 meters) in length and weigh as much as 40 tons (36,000 kilograms). In addition to swallowing small fish, it filters shrimp, krill, and plankton from the water with a mouthful of bony plates called baleen. Humpbacks are found in oceans all over the world. They spend the summer in cold polar seas, then migrate to warmer tropical waters in winter. They are known for producing complex songs—which sound to us like a series of moans, cries, and grunts—that are repeated for hours at a time. We don't know exactly what purpose these songs serve, but we do know that the whales can hear them from hundreds of miles away.

There are several different kinds, or species, of tailorbird. The **common tailorbird** in this book is about five inches (12 ¾ centimeters) long and nests in India and Southeast Asia. Tailorbirds spend most of their time in bushes or trees. They feed on insects, berries, seeds, and flower nectar.

Capuchins make their home in the forests of Central America. They are small monkeys, only about 18 inches

(46 centimeters) long. They eat fruit, leaves, insects, and small animals. Capuchins are among the most intelligent monkeys and are often kept as pets. They were named after the members of a Catholic religious order—the Capuchins—whose brown-hooded robes resemble the brown fur around the monkey's face.

Bighorn sheep live in the mountainous regions of western North America. They are well adapted to life on steep, rocky mountainsides,

moving easily on terrain that few other animals can handle. These sheep feed on grasses, brushy plants, and even cactus. Male bighorn sheep are larger than females, and can weigh as much as 300 pounds (136 kilograms). Males also have thick bony plates on their heads that help them absorb the tremendous impact of their mating duels.

Crows are found on every continent except Antarctica and South America. They are intelligent birds, capable of impressive feats of memory and problem solving. Crows aren't picky eaters. They consume fruit, seeds, insects, frogs, mice, garbage, carrion—even other birds. They can reach 20 inches (51 centimeters) in length, with a wingspan of 36 inches (91 centimeters). In winter, they roost in huge flocks that may include thousands of birds. A flock of these birds is called a "murder" of crows.

The beaver in this book is an **American beaver.** With the exception of arctic and desert habitats, it can be found throughout most of North America. Beavers weigh up to 70 pounds (32 kilograms), making them the world's second largest rodent—only the South American capybara is larger. Beavers are herbivores, feeding on leaves, bark, roots, and water plants. They are important ecosystem engineers. When beavers dam a stream, they create habitat for many wetland plants and animals.

The **mimic octopus** is about two feet (61 centimeters) long. It was discovered by scientists in 1998 in the Indo-Pacific ocean. Like all octopuses, it has ink sacs in its skin that allow it to change its color and pattern. But the mimic octopus also has the unique ability to imitate other animals, most of them venomous. Researchers have reported that it can imitate as many as 15 different sea creatures.

The **reddish egret** is a member of the heron family. It nests on the gulf coasts of the United States and Central America, the Pacific coast of Mexico, and in the Caribbean. This graceful bird stands about 30 inches (76 centimeters) tall, with a wingspan of four feet (122 centimeters). Reddish egrets prefer marshes and shallow lagoons, where they stalk and eat fish, insects, and other small aquatic animals.

Paper wasps make their homes throughout temperate and tropical parts of the world. They are about ¾ inch (2 centimeters) long, and live in colonies of a few hundred insects. Adult wasps feed on pollen, nectar, caterpillars, and other insects. While they are not especially aggressive toward people, paper wasps will sting if their nest is disturbed. Some people experience a dangerous allergic reaction to their venom.

The **barn spider** belongs to a group of spiders known as orb weavers. There are several thousand species of orb weaver, found on every continent except Antarctica. Like all orb weavers, the barn spider spins a large circular web. It is common in the northeastern United States and eastern Canada. Its body is about ¾ inch (2 centimeters) long. Its bite is venomous, but its toxin is mild, so this spider is not dangerous to humans. It traps and eats flies, mosquitoes, and other flying insects. Charlotte, the spider in the book *Charlotte's Web* by E. B. White, was a barn spider.

Bowerbirds get their name from the elaborate nests, or bowers, that male birds construct to attract females. The **satin bowerbird** is about 12 inches (30 centimeters) long.

It lives in the rainforests of eastern Australia and feeds on fruit, leaves, and insects. If a female is suitably impressed with a male's bower and chooses to mate with him, she will not lay her eggs in his bower. Instead, she builds her own nest high in a tree.

Vervet monkeys are native to southern and eastern Africa, though a few have been introduced to Florida and some Caribbean islands. Vervets average 22 inches (56 centimeters) in length and weigh about as much as a housecat. Their diet consists mostly of leaves, seeds, flowers, and fruit. Occasionally they also eat insects, eggs, and small animals. Vervets live in troops of up to fifty. They prefer to stay near trees for safety, but they have adapted to a wide range of habitats, including rainforests, marshes, and grasslands.

Leaf-cutter ants live in colonies that can include millions of insects. A leaf-cutter is either a worker, a soldier, or a queen. Workers collect leaves and tend the colony's underground fungus farm. Soldiers use their big jaws to protect the nest and the workers. There is only one queen. Her job is to lay the eggs—as many as 30,000 a day—that will produce new members of the colony. Workers and soldiers are about a half inch (1¼ centimeters) long. The queen may be twice that size. Leaf-cutter colonies are found in the southern United States and throughout much of Central and South America.

The crocodile in this book is a **Nile crocodile.** It inhabits lakes, rivers, and swamps in central and southern Africa. Reaching 20 feet (6 meters) in length, it is the world's second largest reptile—only the saltwater crocodile is bigger. Nile crocodiles are fierce predators, feeding exclusively on other animals. They will eat birds and fish, but prefer larger prey such as antelopes, zebras, wildebeests—even young elephants and giraffes. Every year, hundreds of people in Africa are killed by crocodiles.

The **nine-banded armadillo** is an armored mammal about 20 inches (51 centimeters) long. It makes its home in the forests and grasslands of the southern United States, Central America, and much of South America. Armadillos are insectivores, feeding primarily on insects. They supplement their diet with frogs, lizards, mice, and other small animals. Armadillos are good swimmers. They can paddle across a stream or hold their breath and walk across on the bottom.

The **ant lion,** the larva of a large flying insect, is about a half inch (1¼ centimeters) long. It is found worldwide, usually in dry, sandy habitats. As an ant lion searches for a spot to dig its trap, it leaves meandering trails in the dirt that resemble doodles drawn on a piece of paper. This has given it the nickname "doodlebug." The ant lion, as its name suggests, eats ants. It also devours beetles, spiders, and other small creatures that tumble into its pit and can't escape.

Because its legs are positioned far back on its body, the **western grebe** moves awkwardly on land. It spends almost its entire life on the water. Even its nest, which is constructed of leaves and sticks, floats on the water's surface. The western grebe is a large bird, about 24 inches (61 centimeters)

long. Its range includes the Pacific coast of Canada, the western and midwestern United States, and Mexico. Its diet consists mostly of fish, but occasionally includes crayfish and worms plucked from the bottom of lakes and stream.

Pythons are not venomous—they squeeze their prey to death. The python in this book is a **reticulated python,** the world's longest snake. There have been reports of pythons more than 30 feet (9 meters) in length, but the longest accurately

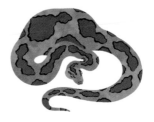

measured snake appears to have been just over 25 feet (7½ meters) long. The reticulated python lives in the forests and grasslands of Southeast Asia, where it attacks and eats a wide range of animals, including birds, rodents, dogs, deer, pigs, crocodiles, and, very rarely, humans.

Bibliography

Alligators and Crocodiles. By Malcolm Penny. Cresent Books, 1991.

Animal Fact File. By Dr. Tony Hare. Checkmark Books, 1999.

Dangerous Animals. Edited by Dr. John Seidensticker and Dr. Susan Lumpkin. Time-Life Books, 1995.

The Life of Birds. By David Attenborough. Princeton University Press, 1998.

Life in the Undergrowth. By David Attenborough. Princeton University Press, 2005.

Nature's Predators. By Michael Bright, Robin Kerrod, and Barbara Taylor. Hermes House, 2003.

The Simon and Schuster Encyclopedia of Animals. Edited by Dr. Philip Whitfield. Simon and Schuster Editions, 1984.

The Way Nature Works. Edited by Robin Rees. Macmillan, 1992.

For Page & Andy and Zoe & Alec

To learn about the making of this book go to stevejenkinsbooks.com/swallowapig.

www.hmhco.com

The text of this book is set in Berthold Akzidenz Grotesk.

The illustrations are torn- and cut-paper collage.

Library of Congress Cataloging-in-Publication Data is on file.

ISBN 978-0-544-31365-1

Manufactured in China

SCP 10 9 8 7 6 5 4 3 2 1

4500529194